W9-AKX-647

VALLEY PARK
DISCARD
ELEMENTARY LIBRARY

ANIMAL TAILS

David M. Schwartz *is an award-winning author of children's books, on a wide variety of topics, loved by children around the world.* Dwight Kuhn's *scientific expertise and artful eye work together with the camera to capture the awesome wonder of the natural world.*

For a free color catalog describing Gareth Stevens Publishing's list of high-quality books and multimedia programs, call 1-800-542-2595 (USA) or 1-800-461-9120 (Canada). Gareth Stevens Publishing's Fax: (414) 225-0377.

Library of Congress Cataloging-in-Publication Data

Schwartz, David M.
    Animal tails / by David M. Schwartz; photographs by Dwight Kuhn.
       p. cm. — (Look once, look again)
    Includes bibliographical references (p. 23) and index.
    Summary: Introduces, in simple text and photographs, the tails belonging to
a mosquito larva, lemur, guppy, tadpole, pig, earwig, and chameleon.
    ISBN 0-8368-2426-1 (lib. bdg.)
    1. Tails — Juvenile literature. [1. Tail. 2. Animals—Habits and behavior.]
I. Kuhn, Dwight, ill. II. Title. III. Series: Schwartz, David M. Look once, look again.
QL950.6.S36   1999
573.9'98—dc21   99-18606

This North American edition first published in 1999 by
Gareth Stevens Publishing
1555 North RiverCenter Drive, Suite 201
Milwaukee, Wisconsin 53212 USA

First published in the United States in 1998 by Creative Teaching Press, Inc., P. O. Box 6017, Cypress, California, 90630-0017.

Text © 1998 by David M. Schwartz; photographs © 1998 by Dwight Kuhn. Additional end matter © 1999 by Gareth Stevens, Inc.

All rights to this edition reserved to Gareth Stevens, Inc. No part of this book may be reproduced, stored in a retrieval system, or transmitted in any form or by any means, electronic, mechanical, photocopying, recording, or otherwise without the prior written permission of the publisher except for the inclusion of brief quotations in an acknowledged review.

Printed in the United States of America

1 2 3 4 5 6 7 8 9 03 02 01 00 99

ANIMAL TAILS

by David M. Schwartz

photographs by Dwight Kuhn

1001113

573.9
SCH

$ 13.10

Animal tails

A SPRINGBOARDS INTO
SCIENCE
SERIES

Gareth Stevens Publishing
MILWAUKEE

This insect begins its life in the water. The insect's tail helps it breathe.

A mosquito larva lives under water. Its tail reaches to the surface so the larva can breathe. Soon it will grow up and fly away from the pond.

A female mosquito uses her tail to lay eggs, but first she must nourish the eggs with blood. Watch out. It could be yours!

Do you recognize this long, ringed tail?
It belongs to an animal found on an island near Africa.

Lemurs live on the island of Madagascar. They have bushy tails and big eyes. This ring-tailed lemur's tail is twice as long as the rest of its body.

This big, bright tail is found on a small fish that is often seen in aquariums.

Male guppies have beautiful tails. Their tails can be red, green, black, white — or a pattern of many colors. Females are attracted to the colorful tails of the male.

As this animal grows bigger, its tail gets smaller!

A tadpole has a long, flat tail to help it move through water. As the tadpole grows and becomes a frog, its tail slowly shrinks. A fully grown frog has no tail at all.

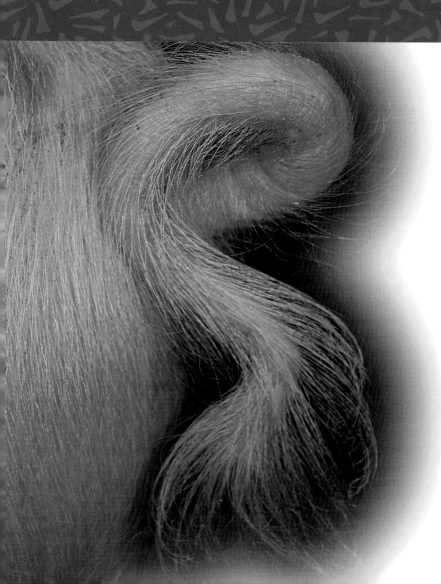

This animal has a curly tail in back and a flat snout in front.

Most pigs' tails are as curly as corkscrews.
They are short and very delicate.

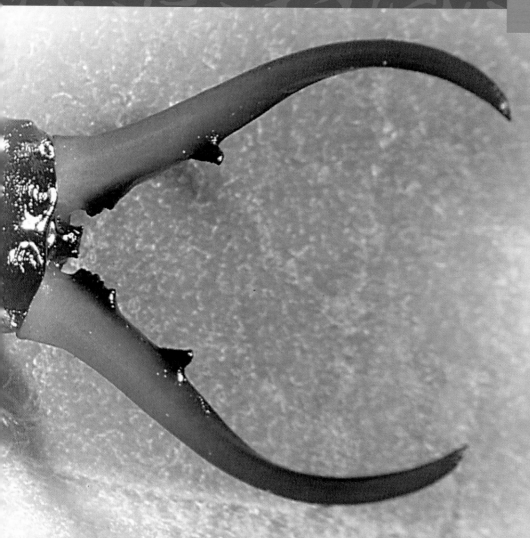

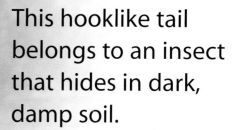

This hooklike tail belongs to an insect that hides in dark, damp soil.

An earwig has two fierce-looking hooks for a tail. The hooks are called cerci (SER-see). An earwig uses its cerci to fight enemies. It also uses them to hold onto its mate. Maybe this is why an earwig is also called a pincher bug.

This tightly curled tail belongs to an animal that changes colors.

VALLEY PARK
ELEMENTARY LIBRARY

A chameleon grasps objects with its tail. When it climbs through trees, the chameleon uses its tail to hold onto branches.
A chameleon can hang upside down by its tail.

A.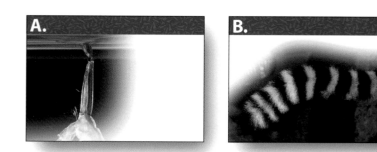

B.

C.

D.

E.

F.

G.

Look closely. Whose tails are these?

LOOK AGAIN

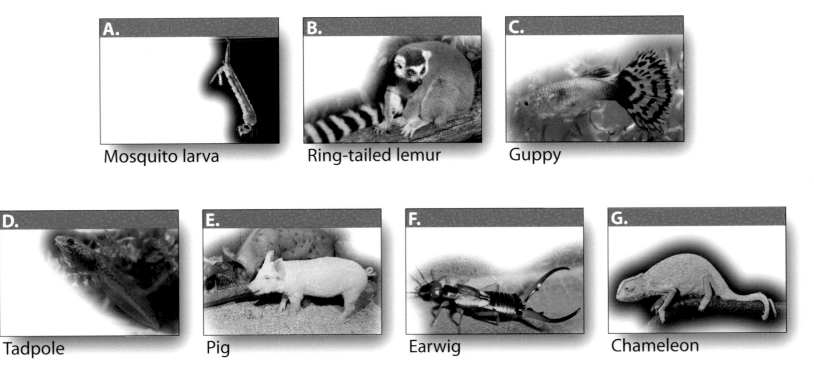

A. Mosquito larva

B. Ring-tailed lemur

C. Guppy

D. Tadpole

E. Pig

F. Earwig

G. Chameleon

How many were you able to identify correctly?

aquarium: a tank or container, usually filled with water, that is used for keeping fish and certain other animals.

attracted: drawn to an object.

breathe: to take air into the body and then force it out.

bushy: thick and shaggy, like fur or hair.

cerci: the pair of hooks on the end of an earwig's body.

chameleon: a small lizard that changes its color to blend in with its surroundings. This camouflage hides it from enemies.

damp: wet; moist.

delicate: easily broken or injured if treated roughly; fragile.

earwig: a kind of insect that has hooks, called cerci, on the end of its body.

fierce-looking: frightening; scary in appearance.

grasp: to grab or hold onto something.

guppy: a small, brightly colored tropical fish that is often kept as a pet.

larva: the wingless stage of an insect's life after it has hatched from an egg and before it becomes an adult.

lemur: an animal related to monkeys that has large eyes and a long, furry tail.

mate (n): the male or female of a pair of animals. The male and female join together for the purpose of producing offspring.

nourish: to provide food for survival.

Go, Fish Tails!

Play a game with a deck of cards you make yourself. With a crayon, draw the body of a fish (without a tail) on a plain white index card. With the same color crayon, draw a matching fish tail on another index card. Make at least ten pairs of cards, using a different animal and color for each pair. Mix up the cards and turn them upside down. You and a friend can then turn two cards over at a time, keeping each matching body and tail. The person with the most cards wins.

Mad about Madagascar

Find Madagascar on a map of the world (first, find Africa, then look off its southeastern coast). Madagascar is home to the ring-tailed lemur and many other unique animals. Find a book in the library or visit a local zoo to learn about other animals that are native to this large island.

Tail Power

The chameleon uses its long tail to hold onto branches and grasp objects. Look through the pictures in this book, and think of all the ways the animals shown use their tails. Make a list of other animals that use their tails in special ways.

"Pin the Tail on the Donkey"

Play the game "Pin the Tail on the Donkey" with family or friends. Place a blindfold on a person's eyes and slowly and carefully turn him or her around in a circle. The blindfolded person then tries to position a tail on a picture of a donkey hanging on the wall. The winner is the person who puts the donkey tail closest to the correct position. "Pin the Tail on the Donkey" is a very old game that your mother or father might have played at birthday parties when they were your age.

More Books to Read

Chameleons: Masters of Disguise. Secrets of the Animal World (series). Eulalia García (Gareth Stevens)
Fish. Wonderful World of Animals (series). Beatrice MacLeod (Gareth Stevens)
Frogs and Toads and Tadpoles, Too. Allan Fowler (Childrens Press)
From Tadpole to Frog. Wendy Pfeffer (HarperCollins)
Mosquitoes. The New Creepy Crawly Collection (series). Enid Broderick Fisher (Gareth Stevens)
Pigs. Animals Are Not Like Us (series). Graham Meadows (Gareth Stevens)
Shadows in the Dawn: Lemurs of Madagascar. Kathryn Lasky (Harcourt Brace)

Videos

All About Tails. (Agency for Instructional Technology)
Chameleons. (New Dimension Media)
The Frog. (Barr Media)

Web Sites

frog.simplenet.com/froggy/
www.hammer.ne.mediaone.net/science/frogs/index.htm

Some web sites stay current longer than others. For further web sites, use your search engines to locate the following topics: *chameleons, earwigs, fish, insects, lemurs, mosquitoes, pigs,* and *tadpoles.*

INDEX

VALLEY PARK

ELEMENTARY LIBRARY